# Madeleine L'Engle

## The Twenty-four Days Before Christmas
### An Austin Family Story

Illustrated by Joe De Velasco

Harold Shaw Publishers
Wheaton, Illinois

### Also by Madeleine L'Engle

An Acceptable Time
Sold Into Egypt
Two-Part Invention
A Cry Like a Bell
A Stone for a Pillow
Many Waters
A House Like a Lotus
And It Was Good
A Severed Wasp
Walking on Water
The Sphinx at Dawn
A Ring of Endless Light
The Anti-Muffins
A Swiftly Tilting Planet
The Weather of the Heart
Ladder of Angels
The Irrational Season
Dragons in the Waters
Summer of the Great-grandmother

Prayers for Sunday
Everyday Prayers
A Wind in the Door
A Circle of Quiet
The Other Side of the Sun
Lines Scribbled on an Envelope
Dance in the Desert
The Young Unicorns
The Journey with Jonah
The Love Letters
The Arm of the Starfish
The Moon by Night
A Wrinkle in Time
Meet the Austins
A Winter's Love
Camilla
And Both Were Young
Ilsa
The Small Rain

Copyright © 1984, Crosswicks Ltd.

Illustrations © 1984 by Joe DeVelasco

ISBN 0-87788-843-4

Printed in the United States of America

---

**Library of Congress Cataloging in Publication Data**

L'Engle, Madeleine.
    The twenty-four days before Christmas.

    Summary: Seven-year-old Vicky Austin recounts the events of the twenty-four days before Christmas, as she prepares for her role as an angel in the Christmas Pageant and prays that her mother will not be in the hospital for Christmas having a new baby.
    1. Children's stories, American. [1. Christmas—Fiction. 2. Family Life—Fiction]
I. DeVelasco, Joe, ill. II. Title.
PZ7.L5385Tw    [Fic]       84-5540
ISBN 0-87788-843-4

---

First printing, August 1984
Second printing, July 1985
Third printing, September 1987
Fourth printing, July 1989
Fifth printing, July 1990

# THE TWENTY-FOUR DAYS BEFORE CHRISTMAS

## December is probably my favorite month.

And on the first day of December we were out of bed before Mother came to call us.

I ran to the window to see if maybe it had snowed during the night. But the ground was still bare, the grass tawny, with a few last leaves fluttering over it. The trees were shaking dark branches against a grey sky.

"Any snow?" Suzy asked. Suzy's my little sister. She's only four, and I've just turned seven. I can read. Of course, so can John. He's ten. I answered, "Not a smidgin. And the sky isn't white enough for snow today. But it doesn't matter—it's the first day of December!"

One of the reasons we love December so is Christmas, not only that Christmas is coming, but that we do something special every single day of the month to prepare for the twenty-fifth day.

John was up and out of the house before Suzy and I were dressed. He has a paper route, every morning before breakfast, and he's allowed to ride all over the village on his bike. I'm the middle Austin and the ugly duckling. If I had more time to remember and think about it I'd be very sad. I'm skinny and as tall as the eight-year-olds and my legs are so long I keep falling. And I was awake early because this was a specially special December for me. I was to be the angel in the Pageant at church on Christmas Eve—the biggest and most wonderful thing that's ever happened to me. I was to wear a golden halo and a flowing white costume and wings, the loveliest wings anyone could imagine. Mother made them.

Suzy is four and she's the baby and all cuddly and beautiful and her hair is curly and the color of sunshine. She has great shining eyes that are the purple-blue of the sky just after sunset. She has a rose-bud for a mouth, and she isn't skinny; she's just right.

We dressed quickly, because even if there wasn't any snow it was cold, and we ran downstairs just as John came in from delivering his papers, his cheeks shiny-red as apples from the cold. The dogs came running in after him, barking, Mr. Rochester, our big brindle Great Dane, and Colette, our little

silver poodle. They're very good friends.

Our kitchen is a big wandery room that turns corners and has unexpected nooks and crannies. In the dining room section in the winter the fire crackles merrily, and this morning the smell of applewood mingled with the smell of pancakes and maple syrup and hot chocolate. One of the cats was sleeping, curled up on a cushion in front of the fire. Our father had already had his breakfast and gone out; he's a doctor and Mother said he'd gone out several hours ago to deliver a baby.

At that we looked at Mother, and the lovely bulge in her dress, and Mother smiled and said, "Daddy thinks the baby should come along sometime the first week in January."

"And then I won't be the baby any more!" Suzy said, "and I'll help you with the new baby."

Suzy's mind flits from thought to thought, just as she herself does, like a butterfly. Now she asked, "What's the surprise for the first day of December?"

It wasn't completely a surprise, because each year it's an Advent calendar, but it's partly a surprise, because it's always a new one. Advent means *coming,* and it's the four weeks that lead up to Christmas. Mother and Daddy read serious things in the evening, and talk about them, a book called *The Four Last Things,* for instance.

This year the calendar was a beautiful one, and had come all the way across the ocean, from Denmark. We take turns every day opening one of the windows to see what surprise picture is waiting behind. The twenty-fourth day when the windows open, they reveal the stable, and Mary and Joseph and the baby.

Today Suzy opened, because she's the youngest and goes first. Inside was a baby angel, who looked just like Suzy.

The next day, the second day of December, we all, even John, even Daddy when he got home from the office, made Christmas cookies. "We'd better make them early this year, just in case."

Just in case the baby comes early.

Mother added, "Babies have a way of keeping mothers too busy for Christmas cookies."

I was born at the end of November, so Mother didn't make any Christmas cookies that year. I always seem to spoil things. I looked out the long kitchen windows at the mountains, thinking: please, don't let me spoil anything this year. Don't let me spoil the Christmas Pageant. Help me to be a good angel. Please.

On the third day of December after the school bus had let John and me off at the foot of the hill, and we'd trudged up the road to our house, Mother got wire and empty tin cans and a few Christmas tree balls. She took strong scissors and cut the tops and bottoms of the cans so that they made stars and curlicues. Then we took thread and hung the Christmas tree balls and the tin designs on the wire, and Mother and John balanced it, and we had made the most beautiful Christmas mobile you could possibly imagine. John got on the ladder and

hung the mobile in the middle of the kitchen ceiling, and it turned and twirled and tinkled and twinkled.

The next day we looked for snow again, but the ground stayed brown, and the trees were dark against the sky. When we went out through the garage to walk down to the school bus, we looked at the big sled, at Daddy's snow shoes, at our ice skates hanging on the wall, at the skis. But though the wind was damp and we had on our warm Norwegian anoraks, we knew it wasn't cold enough for snow. The pond had a thin skin of ice, but not nearly enough for skating, and all that came down from the heavy grey skies was an occasional drizzle that John said might turn into sleet, but not snow.

And the days sped into December. On the fourth day Daddy put a big glimmering golden star over the mantlepiece in the living room. On the fifth day we taped a cardboard Santa Claus with his reindeer up the banisters of the front stairs; it came from England and is very bright and colorful. On the sixth day we strung the merry Norwegian elves across the whole length of the kitchen windows, and Mother said that our Christmas decorations were a real United Nations. On the seventh day we put a tall golden angel above the kitchen mantlepiece. Unlike the Advent calendar angel, this one was much too stately and dignified to look like Suzy, and I sighed because I knew that even with a costume and wings I could never hope to look as graceful and beautiful as the golden angel.

**O**n the eighth day of December I was late getting home because the rehearsal of the Pageant lasted much longer than usual. And it lasted longer because the director couldn't get me in a position that satisfied her. The most awful moment was when I heard her whisper to the assistant director, "I've never seen a seven-year-old be so awkward or ungraceful, but I suppose we really can't recast the angel now."

I clamped my teeth tight shut to try to keep from crying, and the director said, "Don't look so sullen, Vicky. An angel should be joyful, you know."

I nodded, but I didn't dare unclench my teeth. One tear slipped out and trickled down my cheek, but I didn't think anybody saw.

When the rehearsal was over, Mr. Quinn, the minister, drove me home. He hadn't seen the rehearsal and he kept talking about how the Pageant was going to be the best ever, and that I was going to be a beautiful angel. If he'd been at the rehearsal he wouldn't have said that.

The Advent surprise for that day was to have the Christmas mugs at dinner, the mugs that look like Santa Claus. But I still felt like crying, and the cheerful Santa Claus face didn't cheer me up at all. After we had baths and were in our warm pajamas and ready for bed, we stood around the piano singing Advent carols, but I had such a big lump in my throat that I couldn't sing.

Daddy put his arm around me. "What's the matter with my girl?"

Two tears slipped out of my eyes, and I told him about the rehearsal and what the director had said. He told me that he and Mother would help me to look and move more like an angel. "You can be a lovely angel, Vicky, but you'll have to work at it."

"I'll work. I promise."

On the ninth day of Advent we hung the Christmas bells from the beams in the living room, and then Mother worked with me on being an angel. She had me walk all over the house with a volume of the encyclopedia on my head. When I was finally able to walk all around without the encyclopedia falling, Mother showed me how to stand with my feet in ballet position, and how to hold my arms so they didn't look all elbows.

On the tenth day of December Mother got the cuddly Santa Claus doll out of the attic, and told Suzy and me we could take turns taking it to bed at night. I thought of the pageant, and said, "Suzy can have it. May I take the *Shu* to *Sub* volume of the encyclopedia to bed with me?"

Mother understood. "Yes. And now put it on your head and try walking up the front stairs and down the back stairs."

Each time I did it I managed more steps without having to catch the encyclopedia. Suzy went to bed with the cuddly Santa Claus doll. I put the *Shu* to *Sub* volume under my pillow.

On the eleventh day the director beamed at me and said, "That was *much* better, Vicky. I think you're going to be all right after all. Now let's try it again. *Good,* Vicky, GOOD."

I was happy when I got home and Mother gave me a hug, and John said, "I don't know why anybody ever thought you couldn't do it. I knew you could."

Suzy jumped up and down and said, "What're we going to

do for Advent today?"

Mother suggested, "Let's make a Christmas chandelier." We took the wire mesh lettuce basket and filled it with the Christmas decorations which were just a tiny bit broken but not shattered. We hung one of the prettiest, shiniest decorations on the bottom of the lettuce basket, and then Mother and John fitted the basket over the front hall light so that it glittered and sparkled with the color of all the Christmas baubles.

And I walked up and down the front hall with the encyclopedia, *Shu* to *Sub,* balanced on my head; I tried to look at the Christmas chandelier out of the corner of my eye, but when I looked up the encyclopedia slipped and I caught it just before it landed on the floor.

**O**n the twelfth day of December not only did it not snow, it did rain. Rain poured in great torrents from the sodden skies and the gutters spouted like fountains. After school Mother discovered that we'd eaten up all the first batch of Christmas cookies, so we made more.

On the thirteenth the skies were all washed clean and the sun was out and we had a Pageant rehearsal. The director surprised me by saying, "Vicky, dear, you're doing so well that we've decided to give you some lines for the scene where you

appear with the shepherds. Do you think you can memorize
them?"

I nodded happily. It may be hard for me to walk without
tripping up, and to stand still without being all sharp corners
and angles, but memorizing things is easy for me.

The director explained, "These are the angel lines from an
old play in the Chester Cycle. The Chester Cycle is a group of
plays written in the Middle Ages in England, to be performed
in the Cathedral in Chester, so we think it's very appropriate

for the Pageant. By the way, we miss your mother in the choir."

I explained, "It's because of the new baby, you know."

"Isn't that nice! I wonder if she'll be in the hospital for Christmas? Now here are your lines, dear. Read them slowly and clearly."

I read. Slowly and clearly. But I hardly heard myself. Mother in the hospital for Christmas? I knew Mother'd go to the hospital to have the baby, just as she did for John and me and Suzy. But not for Christmas Eve! Not for Christmas day!

"Good, dear," the director was saying. "Read it once more."

I read.

> *Shepherds, of this sight*
> *Be not afright,*
> *For this is God's night.*
> *To Bethlehem now hie.*
> *There shall ye see and sight*
> *That Christ was born tonight*
> *To save all mankind.*

If Mother was in the hospital it wouldn't be Christmas. Christmas is the *whole* family hanging up stockings, and Daddy reading *The Night Before Christmas* and Saint Luke, and Mother singing everybody to sleep with her guitar and carols. What about the stocking presents Christmas morning in Mother's and Daddy's big bed? What about running downstairs all together to see the presents under the tree?

What about—what about—everything?

Who would cook the Christmas dinner? Make the stuffing? Roast the turkey? Fix the cranberry sauce? What about putting out cocoa and cookies for Santa Claus the very last thing on Christmas Eve? What about—what about— everything?

"That's very good, dear," the director approved. "You speak beautifully. Now read it again, just a little bit more slowly this time. Do you think you can memorize it for tomorrow?"

I nodded numbly. Somehow or other I managed to do everything the director told me, but all I could think was— Mother *has* to be home for Christmas!

Daddy picked me up after rehearsal that afternoon. As soon as he had the car started, I asked, "Daddy, Mother isn't going to be in the hospital for Christmas is she?"

He answered quietly, "It's a distinct possibility."

I shouted, "But she can't be!"

Daddy said calmly, "According to our calculations, the baby's due about the first of January, but babies don't always arrive exactly on schedule. John, for instance, was three weeks late, and you were exactly on time. Suzy was a few days early."

"But—"

"Who knows, the baby may decide to come early enough so that Mother'll be home for Christmas. Or it mightn't be till the new year. But we have to accept the fact that there's a chance that Mother'll be in the hospital over Christmas."

"Let's not *have* the baby!" I cried. "If Mother has to be in the hospital on Christmas I don't want the baby!"

"Here, here," Daddy said, "that's no way to talk."

"There are enough of us already." I choked over a sob. "Do we have to have the baby, Daddy?"

"Of course we do. We all want the baby. This isn't like you, Vicky Austin."

"What about Christmas dinner?" I wailed.

"At the last count," Daddy said, "we'd had seventeen invitations for dinner."

It kept getting worse and worse. "But we can't go *out* for Christmas dinner! I'd rather have cornflakes and have them at home!"

Daddy turned the car up the hill to the house. "I quite agree with you there, Vic. I've turned down all the invitations. If Mother's in the hospital I think you and John and Suzy and I can manage Christmas dinner, don't you? And I'll let you in on a secret: Mother already has a turkey stuffed and roasted and in the freezer. All we have to do is thaw it and heat it up in the oven."

I hiccuped tiredly. "Well. All right. But it won't be Christmas if Mother isn't with us."

Daddy changed the subject. He's very good about knowing when to do that. "I heard you saying your angel lines, Vicky. We're going to be very proud of you on Christmas Eve."

When we got home, Mother and John and Suzy were in the kitchen, stuffing dates. John shouted, "Vicky! There's snow forecast for tomorrow!"

On the fourteenth day of December three snowflakes fell. Exactly three. I counted them. They fell while we were out in the woods picking berries and ground pine for Christmas decorations.

On the fifteenth day of December Daddy and John got out the ladder, and Mother and Suzy and I untangled the long strings of outdoor lights and we trimmed the big Norway spruce.

"We're going to do quite a few things early this year," Daddy explained, "because of not knowing just when the baby is going to decide to be born." I didn't want to think about that.

At night the spruce shone so brightly that it could be seen all the way from the main road at the bottom of the hill.

And that afternoon Mother came to pick me up after rehearsal and the director said, just as though I couldn't hear, "I must admit to you, Mrs. Austin, that I was a little unsure of Vicky for the first few rehearsals. She's the youngest angel we've ever chosen and I had grave doubts as to whether or not she could do it. But now I think she's going to be the very best we've ever had, and she knows her lines perfectly."

One part of me blazed with happiness. Another part thought sadly—It won't be Christmas if Mother isn't home.

As we drove away from the church and turned down the main road, Mother pointed to the hilltop where our big white house perches, and I could see a little triangle of light that was the outdoor Christmas tree. And another awful thought struck me. "Mother! If you're in the hospital you won't be able to see me being the angel!"

"That's true."

"But I *want* you to see me!"

"I want to see you, too."

"In the olden days people didn't have to go to hospitals to have babies. They had them at home."

"So they did," Mother agreed. "But even if I had the baby at home, I couldn't come see you being the angel."

"Why not?"

"Brand new babies need a lot of attention," Mother said, "and they can't be taken out in the cold. I was pretty tied down at Christmas time the year you were born."

"But I was *born!*" I cried. "And you were home for Christmas. You didn't go off and leave John and Suzy alone. Oh, I forgot. Suzy wasn't born. Anyhow, Mother, please could you ask the baby to wait till after Christmas?"

"I can ask," Mother said, "but I wouldn't count on it. What shall we do today for our Special Thing?"

"Let's make the wreath for the front door."

"Good idea. We've got lots of ground pine and berries left over, and I saved all the pine cones we gilded and silvered last year. When we get home you can run up to the attic and get them."

On the sixteenth day of December John listened to the weather forecast before breakfast and snow was predicted again. The sky had the white look that means it is heavy with snow. John and I were so pleased we ran almost the whole of the mile down the hill to wait for the school bus. A cold raw wind was blowing and we huddled into our parkas.

After school I had a rehearsal. So did John, because he's singing in the choir, and this is the first time that the cast of the Pageant and the choir have worked together.

I tried hard to walk the way I did with the *Shu* to *Sub* encyclopedia on my head, and to move my arms as though they were the graceful arms of a tree in spring and not the bare brittle branches of a tree in December. I remembered all my lines in my heart as well as my mind, and Mother had worked with me to make each word ring out clear and pure as a bell. Everybody seemed pleased, and John pounded me on the back and told me I was a whiz. The choir director congratulated me, just as though I were a grown up, and told me that everybody was going to miss Mother in the choir, and I was forced once again to remember that Mother might not be home for Christmas. John asked the choir director if he thought it would snow, but he shook his head. "It's turned too cold for snow."

Mr. Irving, the choir director drove us home and stopped in for a cup of tea. A big box of holly and mistletoe had arrived from our cousins on the West coast, so John and Daddy hung the mistletoe on one of the beams in the living room.

After Mr. Irving had left, we opened the day's Christmas cards the way we always do, taking turns, so that each card can be looked at and admired and appreciated.

John remarked, "Some people just rip open their cards in the post office. I bet the kids never see them at all. I'm glad we don't do it that way."

"Everybody's different, John," Mother said. "That's what makes people interesting."

"Well, nobody else I know does something every day during Advent the way we do. What's our Special Thing for today?"

"Oh, I think the holly and the mistletoe's plenty. Start setting the table, Vic. It's nearly time to eat."

The days toward Christmas flew by, and still there was no snow. And no baby. And rehearsals went well and I was happy about the way being the angel was going, and so was the director.

On the seventeenth of December we hung our collection of doll angels all over the house, and on the eighteenth we put the Christmas candle in the big kitchen window. On the nineteenth we made Christmas cards, with colored paper and sparkle and cutouts from last year's Christmas cards.

On the twentieth we put up the crêche. This is one of the most special of all the special things that happen before Christmas. Over the kitchen counter is a cubby hole with two shelves. Usually mugs are kept in the bottom shelf, and the egg cups and the pitcher that is shaped like a cow on the top shelf. But for Christmas, Mother makes places for these in one of the kitchen cabinets. On the top shelf goes the wooden stable and the shepherds. Tiny wax angels fly over the stable. A dove sits on the roof. The ox and the ass and all the

barnyard animals are put in, one by one, everybody taking turns. There is even a tiny pink pig with three little piglets, from a barnyard set John got one year for his birthday. There is a sheep dog and a setting hen and a grey elephant the size of the pig. Some people might think the elephant doesn't belong, but the year I was born Daddy gave him to John, and he's been part of the crêche ever since, along with two monkeys and a giraffe and a polar bear. Mary and Joseph will be put in on the morning of Christmas Eve, and then, when

we get home from Church on Christmas Eve night, Daddy
puts in the baby Jesus, and reads the nativity story from St.
Luke.

On the bottom shelf we put the wise men with their
camels and their camel-keeper. We make a hill out of cotton,
which is a little hard to balance the camels on, but when
we're finished it really looks as though the train of camels was
climbing up a long weary road towards the Christ child. On
Twelfth Night they'll have finished their journey and join the
shepherds and the animals in the stable.

Last of all Daddy put the star up above the stable and
fixed the light behind it. On Christmas Eve we'll turn off all

the other lights in the house, so all you can see is the lovely
light from the star shining on the stable and the Holy Family
and the angels and the animals.

On the twenty-first day of December we went with Daddy
into the woods to get the Christmas tree. Mother stayed home,
because she was feeling tired and heavy, but the rest of us
tramped through the woods, including the dogs and cats. It
was Suzy who found the perfect tree this time, just the right
size and shape for the living room, with beautiful firm

branches all around. Daddy and John took turns sawing, and we all helped carry it home, because the tree was tall, and heavy.

Daddy said, "Tomorrow's Sunday, so we'll trim the tree a little ahead of time to get it ready for Santa Claus and to make sure Mother's here to help."

John asked, "You really don't think the baby's going to wait till after Christmas, Daddy?"

"I rather doubt it. Every indication is that this baby is going to be early. Now, kids, we'll put the tree carefully into the garage till tomorrow."

That night I woke up, very wide awake. I knew it wasn't anywhere near morning because the light was still on in Mother's and Daddy's bedroom. After a few minutes I got up, softly, so as not to wake Suzy. I put on my bathrobe and slippers and tiptoed down to the kitchen. The dogs came pattering out to meet me, wagging their tails. One of the cats meowed at the head of the cellar stairs. I put my finger to my lips and said, "Shh! Everybody go back to sleep."

It wasn't quite dark in the kitchen because the embers in the fireplace were still glowing, and the night light was on. Mother and Daddy must have gone up to bed just a little while ago. I tiptoed over to the crêche, climbed on one of the kitchen

stools, and turned on the light behind the star. The manger was empty, waiting for Mary and Joseph and the baby. They were still in their white cardboard box. I opened the lid and looked in, then closed the lid and put the box back.

Instead of feeling all full of anticipation the way I usually do, I felt heavy. I thought—I don't want Mother to be in the hospital for Christmas. I want her to be home. I'd give anything if she could be home. But I don't have anything to give. Anyhow, God doesn't expect us to give anything in order for him to love us. And least not a thing. Just ourselves.

I sighed again. And thought—Mother says we should never try to make bargains with God. That isn't the way God works. But I'd give up anything, even being the angel, if Mother could be home for Christmas.

I sat looking at the empty crib in the stable until I got sleepy.

On the twenty-second of December when we were all home from Sunday school and church, Mother made hamburgers and milkshakes for lunch. Then Suzy and I helped with the dishes and Mother put on a carol record and we all sang "O Come, O Come, Emmanuel." Daddy and John brought in the tree from the garage and set it firmly in a bucket of wet sand. The big boxes of Christmas decorations were brought down from the attic. First of all Daddy got on the ladder and he and John put on the lights, and the angel at the top of the tree. The angel is wearing white, with feathery sparkly wings; it's the angel mother used to copy my costume. It was almost as though Daddy was putting a tiny *me* up on top of the tree.

I thought of the night before, and how I'd thought I'd be willing to give up being the angel if only Mother could be home for Christmas, but I couldn't give up being the angel without upsetting the whole Christmas Pageant, and anyhow, that kind of thing isn't an offering to God. As our Grandfather once told us, you can't offer anything less than yourself to God; anything less is a bribe, and bribing God is foolish, to say the least. I didn't really understand all of this. Grandfather's a theologian, though, and I was sure he was right.

Mother looked at me and said, "What's the matter, Vicky?"

"Nothing. May I put on some of the breakables this year?"

Suzy was given a box of unbreakable ornaments to go on the lowest branches of the tree. Mother smiled and handed me a beautiful little glass horn that really makes a musical sound. I blew it, and then I let Suzy blow it, too. We all worked together until the tree was shimmering with beauty.

I took a gold glass bell with a gentle tinkle and hung it on the highest branch I could reach. When the last decoration was hung from the tree and we'd all exclaimed (as usual) that it was the most beautiful tree ever, John ran around and turned out all the other lights so that the Christmas tree shone alone in the darkness. We all stood around it, very still, admiring it, and I was peaceful and happy. For a moment I forgot about being the angel. I even forgot about the baby.


On the twenty-third day of December when I went to the church for dress rehearsal it finally began to snow. Everybody began to clap and shout with glee, and we kept running to the doors to look at the great feather flakes fluttering from a soft, fluffy sky. Finally the director got cross at us and ordered everyone inside, and Mr. Irving made a big discord on the organ.

In the Sunday school rooms several mothers helped us get into costume. I was dressed early, and Mrs. Irving, who dressed me, said, "Vicky dear, if you stand around here in this mob your wings are going to get crushed. Go sit quietly in the back of the church until we're ready to start the run-through."

I went, holding my wings carefully, through the big doors and half way down the nave. The church was transformed with pine boughs and candles. The candles wouldn't be lit until just before the Christmas Eve service, but there was a spotlight shining on the manger. The girl who played Mary came and stood beside me, a high school senior and very, very grown up. She wore a pale blue gown and a deep blue robe. She dropped one hand lightly on my shoulder.

"Some of us thought it was funny, such a little kid being chosen for the angel, and at first we thought you were going to be awful and ruin everything. But Mr. Quinn promised us you wouldn't, and now I think you're going to be the best thing in the Pageant, I honestly do." Then she went and sat by the manger. She sat very still, her head bowed. She didn't seem like a high school senior any more. She seemed to belong in Bethlehem. Protecting my wings, I sat down in one of the pews. And for a while, I, too, seemed to be in Bethlehem.

Then the director called out time for the run-through to begin, and everything was hustle and bustle again. The choir in their red cassocks and white surplices lined up for the processional. I was shown into the corner behind the organ, from where I was to make my first entrance.

Everything went smoothly. I even managed to walk as though I had *Shu* to *Sub* on my head. My arms felt like curves instead of angles. My words were as bell-like as Mother'd been able to make them. At the final tableau I stood by the manger, and I felt shining with joy.

After the choir had recessed and the spotlight had faded on the nativity scene, the director and Mr. Irving congratulated everybody. "It was beautiful, just beautiful!" The mothers who had helped with the costumes and had stayed to watch echoed, "Beautiful! Beautiful!" Except for the fathers, almost everybody who was going to be at church on Christmas Eve was already there.

The director gave me a big smile. "Vicky, you were just perfect. Don't change one single thing. Tomorrow evening for the performance do it just exactly the way you did today."

Daddy picked John and me up on his way home from the office. It was still snowing, great, heavy flakes. The ground was already white. Daddy said, "I'm glad I got those new snow tires after all."

John said, "You see, Daddy, we *are* going to have a white Christmas after all."

When we woke up on Christmas Eve morning we ran to the windows. Not only was the ground white, but we couldn't even see the road. Mother said the snow plow went through at five o'clock so the farmers could get the milk out, and Daddy had followed the milk trucks, but the road had already filled in again.

We ate breakfast quickly, put on snow suits, and ran out to play. The snow was soft and sticky, the very best kind for making snowmen and building forts. We spent the morning making a Christmas snowman, and started a fort around him. John is good at cutting blocks out of snow like an Eskimo. We weren't nearly finished, though, when Mother called us in for lunch.

After lunch Suzy said, "I might as well go upstairs and have my nap and get it over with." We have to have naps on Christmas Eve if we want to stay after the Pageant for the Christmas Eve service. Suzy is very business-like about things like naps. Mother looked a little peculiar, but she didn't say anything, and Suzy went upstairs to bed, taking a book. She can't read, but she likes looking at pictures. Mother lit the kitchen fire and sat in front of it to read to John and me. We were just settled and comfortable when the phone rang. Mother answered it. We listened.

"Yes, I was afraid of that . . . Of course . . . They'll be disappointed, but they'll have to understand." She hung up and turned to John and me.

"What's the matter?" John asked.

Mother said, "The Pageant's been called off because of the blizzard, and so has the Christmas Eve service."

"But *why?*" John demanded.

Mother looked out the windows. "How do you think anybody could travel in this weather, John? We're completely snowed in. The road men are concentrating on keeping the main roads open, but all the side roads are unusable. That means that about three quarters of the village is snowed in just like us. I'm sorry about the angel, Vicky. I know it's a big disappointment to you, but remember that lots of other children are disappointed, too."

I looked over at the crêche, with Mary and Joseph now in their places, and the manger still empty and waiting for the baby Jesus. "Well, I guess lots worse things could happen." I thought—If this means Mother will be home for Christmas . . .

And then I thought—Blizzards can stop pageants, but they can't stop babies, and if the baby starts coming she'll have to go to the hospital anyhow . . .

"You're a good girl to be so philosophical," Mother said.

But I didn't really think I was being philosophical.

John said, "Anyhow, it looks as though the baby's going to wait till after Christmas."

Mother answered, "Let's hope so."

John pressed his nose against the window until the pane

steamed up. "How's Daddy going to get home?"

It seemed to me that Mother looked anxious as she said, "I must admit I'm wondering about that myself."

"But it's Christmas Eve!" John said. "He *has* to get home!"

All Mother said was, "He'll do the best he can. At least I'm the only maternity case on his list right now."

In all my worrying about Mother not being home for Christmas, it had never occurred to me that Daddy mightn't be. Even when he's been called off on an emergency, he's always been around for most of the time. But if the blizzard was bad enough to call off church it was maybe bad enough so Daddy couldn't get up the long steep hill that led to the village.

When it began to get dark, Suzy woke up, all pink from sleep, and hurried downstairs. She was very cross when Mother told her that the Pageant and the Christmas Eve service had been called off. "I needn't have slept so long after all! And I wanted to see Vicky be the angel!"

Mother answered, "We all did, Suzy."

Suzy stamped. "I'm *mad* at the old blizzard."

Mother laughed. "That's not going to stop the snow. And remember, you've been looking for snow every day. Now you've got it. With a vengeance. This is the worst blizzard I remember in years."

John lit the candle in the window and flicked the switch

that turns on the outdoor Christmas tree and the light over the garage door. Then we all looked out the windows. The only way you could tell where the road used to be is by the five little pines at the edge of the lawn, and by the birches across the road. The outdoor Christmas tree was laden with snow, and the lights shone through and dropped small pools of color on the white ground. The great flakes of snow were still falling as heavily as ever, soft and starry against the darkness.

"I guess Daddy'll have to spend the night at the hospital," John said.

Mother came to the window and looked over our heads. "No car can possibly get up that road."

Suzy asked, "What're we going to have for dinner?"

Mother turned from the window. "I think I'll just take hamburger out of the freezer . . ." I thought she looked worried.

I stayed by the window. —Please let Daddy get home. Please let Daddy get home.

But I knew Mother was right, and a car couldn't possibly get up the road, even with new snow tires and chains.

—Please, God, I'm not bargaining, I'm not bribing or anything, I'm just asking, Please let Daddy get home. If I knew how to offer my whole self I would, but I don't know how, so please let Daddy get home, please let . . .

Then, just as the words began to jumble themselves up in my mind, I saw something in the wide expanse of snow, somewhere near where the curve of the road ought to be. A light. "Mother! John! Suzy!" They all came running to the window.

"It's a flashlight," John said.

"Snowshoes!" Mother cried. "John, run to the garage and see if Daddy took his snowshoes!"

John hurried to the kitchen door and in a minute came back, grinning happily. "They're gone."

The light came closer and closer and soon we could see Daddy, his head and shoulders covered with snow. His snowshoes moved steadily and regularly over the white ground. We ran tumbling out to the garage and flung our arms around him, and the dogs jumped up on him and barked in greeting.

"Whoa!" he said. "Let me get my snowshoes off!" He handed the snowshoes to John, who hung them up. Then he stamped his feet and shook, and snow tumbled off him. The dogs dashed out into the snow, came whirling back into the garage, and shook off even more snow. "Come along," Daddy said. "Let's get in out of the cold."

When we got indoors Daddy kissed Mother. She leaned her head against his shoulder. "I was afraid you wouldn't be able to get home."

Daddy said, "You didn't think I'd leave you now, did you?"

And Mother said, "I've been having contractions off and on all day. Oh, I am so glad you're home!"

Daddy put another log on the fire. Outdoors the snow was

still falling. Indoors it was warm and cozy. The star lit up the little stable, and Daddy went to the white cardboard box and took out the tiny wax figure of the baby. "I think we can put him in the manger, now."

Mother said, "We might as well have the reading, now, too, because this is all the Christmas Eve service we're going to get."

John went into the living room and turned on the Christmas tree lights so that there was the beauty of the Christmas tree indoors and the Christmas tree outdoors, and Daddy sat by the fire and read us the Christmas story. I looked at the angel on top of the indoor Christmas tree and I felt peaceful and happy.

When we'd finished dinner and were nearly through with the dishes, Mother gave a funny little gasp and said to Daddy, "How are you going to get me to the hospital?"

Daddy laughed. "Upstairs is as far as I'm going to get you tonight." He looked at us. "Children, I'm going to ask you to finish the dishes and clean up the kitchen." Suddenly he sounded like a doctor, not just Daddy. "John, put on a full kettle to boil. Blizzards don't ask anybody when they should come, and neither do babies."

He put his arm about Mother and they went upstairs.

"What about dessert?" Suzy asked. "We were going to have dessert after we'd done the dishes."

"If you're really interested in dessert I'll get you some ice cream out of the freezer," John said.

After all, Suzy is a very little girl. She ate a large bowl of ice cream.

When the kitchen was all cleaned up, Daddy came downstairs. He carried the Christmas stockings and he told us to hang them carefully at the living room fireplace. "You'd be staying up late tonight anyhow, so please just be good. Vicky, keep that kettle hot for me, and feed the cats and put them down in the cellar for the night."

The snow beat against the windows. The wind rattled the shutters. In spite of her nap Suzy got sleepy and curled up on the living room sofa. I went to the stove. "I'd better make the cocoa to put on the mantlepiece with the cookies for Santa Claus."

"Make enough for us while you're at it," John said.

We drank two, then three cups of cocoa. We tiptoed out to the storeroom where we'd hidden our presents for Mother and Daddy and put them under the tree. Time seemed to stretch out and out and Daddy didn't come back downstairs. The dogs lay in front of the fire and snored. Suddenly Mr. Rochester, the great Dane, pricked up his ears. John and I listened, but we didn't hear anything. At the top of the cellar stairs a cat meowed. Mr. Rochester sat up and raised his head; his tail thumped against the floor.

Then we did hear something, something unmistakable, loud and clear. A cry. A baby's cry.

I started to get up, but John said, "Wait."

In a little while Daddy came bounding down the stairs. He was beaming. "You have a little brother, children!" He took the kettle and hurried back up the stairs, calling, "You can come up in a few minutes. Wait."

The baby cried again, a lusty yell.

I went to the crêche. The light from the star shone down on the stable. The elephant and the pig and her piglets seemed to have moved in closer. The baby lay on his bed of straw.

"Listen." John held up his hand. Across the fields came the sound of the clock in the church steeple striking midnight. "Let's wake Suzy up, and tell her."

Suzy sleeps soundly and it took us a long time to wake her properly. By the time she realized what had happened, Daddy came back downstairs.

"You can come up now, for just a minute, children. But Mother's tired, and the baby's asleep, so be very quiet."

We tiptoed up the stairs and into the big bedroom. Mother was lying in the big bed and smiling. In the crook of her arm was a little bundle. We tiptoed closer. The bundle was our baby brother. His face was all puckered and rosy. His eyes were closed tight. He had a wisp of dampish hair. He had a tiny bud of a mouth. One little fist was close to his cheek. We stood and stared at him. We were too excited and awed to speak.

Mother asked, "Isn't he beautiful?" and we all nodded.

Then Daddy shooed us out. "All right. Time for bed, everybody."

John went off to his room, and Suzy and I to ours. When we had undressed and brushed our teeth and Suzy was in bed, I stood at the window. The snow had stopped. The ground was a great soft blanket of white, broken by the dark lines of trees and the gay colors of the outdoor tree. The sky was dark and clear and crusted with stars. I watched and watched and there was one star that was brighter and more sparkling than any of the others.

The Christmas star.

Mother was home. Daddy was home. Our baby brother was home. We were all together.

I whispered, "Thank you."

And the light shone right into my heart.